# The Rosicrucian Manifestos

*Fama Fraternitatis*

*Confessio Fraternitatis*

*The Chymical Wedding of Christian Rosenkreutz*

*Positio Fraternitatis Rosae Crucis*

Published by:     The Rosicrucian Collection®
Greenwood Gate, Blackhill
Crowborough  TN6 1XE
United Kingdom.

Tel:     +44-(0)1892-653197
Fax:     +44-(0)1892-667432
Email:     sales@amorc.org.uk
UK Website:     www.amorc.org.uk
International Website:  www.amorc.org

Copyright:     The Supreme Grand Lodge of AMORC, Inc.
© 2006.
All Rights Reserved

ISBN:     0 952 64203 4

© 2006
Printed and bound by AMORC Services Ltd.

# CONTENTS

# An Introduction to the Chymical Wedding

# An Introduction to the
# Chymical Wedding

*(Foxcroft English translation, 1690)*

PUBLISHED IN 1616 AT STRASBOURG as *Die Chymische Hochzeit des Christiani Rosenkreutz*, the third Manifesto is an altogether different document from the preceding two. It essentially describes in narrative form an inner journey of personal transformation. This is often referred to as spiritual alchemy. Although we see the process in this story as physical activity, allegorically it represents the changes occurring to the inner self of the main character, Christian Rosenkreutz, who narrates it in the first person, allowing us to identify with the character.

In the opening paragraph we find Christian Rosenkreutz in an act of private communion with the Master Jesus. The whole tone here conveys to the reader the great humility and spiritual nature of this person and we are left in no doubt that this is a man of special qualities. Suddenly an unexpected "tempest" whips up but he persists in his meditation when, after being touched on the shoulder, he is confronted by a divine messenger who places a letter upon the table in front of him and with a mighty blast on a trumpet, disappears.

The letter turns out to be an invitation to the wedding of a King and Queen who live in a large castle although he has no idea where this is situated. However, a little later we learn that the invitation is not entirely unexpected and had been earnestly desired and prayed for as a result of a vision experienced seven years before. But its arrival has now prompted him toward self examination and filled him with lack of confidence in his worthiness to accept it. In such a frame of mind he decides, after prayer, to get some sleep in the hope that through dreams, his inner self might instruct him on the course he should take.

He does indeed dream; he finds himself in a dungeon with many men fettered with chains. A trumpet sounds from above and a cover is opened; from this a rope is lowered seven times. Our character manages to grasp it at the sixth lowering and then helps to pull it up during the seventh, assisting those who were hanging onto it. After the cover is slammed shut Rosenkreutz displays emotion at the sound of those left behind. An "ancient matron" then writes the names of those redeemed in a golden-yellow book and gives them each a piece of gold bearing the symbol of the rising sun and the letters DLS. A blast from a trumpet wakens our character and with the dream being so vivid, he still feels the wounds he received in it.

With his faith renewed however, he prepares for the journey, donning a white linen coat, a red ribbon over his shoulder and in his hat, four red roses so that he will be recognised as a brother of the Rosy Cross. He also carries bread, salt and water for food. Before he leaves, dressed in his "wedding garment," he kneels down and vows that any knowledge he acquires will not be misused but put toward the service of his neighbour and the spreading of God's name.

So begins a seven day journey of initiation accompanied in part by others of different temperament and spiritual worth.

## Sevenfold Architecture

There is a sevenfold structure[1] in this narrative that is nearly impossible for the reader to miss since it occurs throughout the text. The most obvious example is the seven days over which other sevenfold events happen. Some examples of these are:

| | |
|---|---|
| First Day: | The rope is lowered seven times in the dream sequence. |
| Third Day: | Seven weights are used to test the candidates' worth; these equate to the seven virtues of wisdom, justice, temperance, fortitude, faith, hope and love. |
| Fourth Day: | The Comedy play with seven acts. |
| | The Altar and its six ritual objects. |
| | The seven ships along with the seven verses of the Sirens' song. |
| | The beheading of seven people in the "Wedding" ceremony: the Bride and Bridegroom, the two Kings and their Queens and also the Moor. |
| Sixth Day: | The ascent of the seven floors or levels of the Tower of Olympus. |

## Other Sevenfold Elements Include:

The seven *tests* with six of them on the first day:

1. His resolve and courage are tested by the invitation.
2. He gives up his bread at the testing of the four ways.
3. He gives up his water at the First Portal.
4. He gives up his salt at the Second Portal.
5. He gives up his coat and outer garments at the Third Portal.
6. In the Hall of Guests he decides to stay behind because he has no confidence in his worthiness.
7. On the second day he is tested at the weighing scene.

The seven *items* he has with him at the start of the journey: bread, water, salt, outer garments, his hair (he is tonsured on the second day), the four roses and his hat.

The seven *tokens* or gifts he receives:

1. On the first day, a token of gold with the rising sun embossed on one side and the letters DLS on the other.[2]
2. On the second day, a token from the First Porter with the letters SC appearing on it.
3. Again on the second day, a token from the Second Porter with the letters SM appearing on it
4. And once again on the second day, the Third Porter gives him a further token with the letters SPN.
5. On the third day, he is presented with a medallion of the Golden Fleece on behalf of the Bridegroom following the weighing scene.
6. On the fourth day, another medallion of the Golden Fleece but set about with precious stones which also has a medal of gold suspended from it. On one side of this are the sun and moon in opposition to each other while on the reverse is inscribed a short verse.
7. On the seventh day, as a Knight of the Golden Stone, Rosenkreutz is presented a medal of gold, on one of which is AR. NAT. MI. while on the other is TEM. NA. F.

The seven rooms or areas within the Castle to which Christian Rosenkreutz is admitted:

1. The outer gates and ante-chamber where he is tonsured.
2. The Dining Hall where he meets guests and also where the weighing scene happens.
3. The Garden where those guests that fail the test of weighing are ridiculed and scourged. This is also the place where the mock burial occurs.
4. The Library and the room with the terrestrial globe.
5. The Royal winding stairs leading to the Hall of the Wedding.
6. The House of the Sun in which the Comedy play is enacted.
7. The underground chamber of Venus.

## Three Levels of Working

There are three consecutive levels upon which the allegory is set. The first one is the outer, mundane world where we first encounter Christian Rosenkreutz. Here he is a member of the Fraternity of the Rose Cross. The second is the Castle of the Bridegroom where he becomes a Knight of the Golden Fleece. And finally there is the Tower of Olympus where he receives the ultimate accolade, that of a Knight of the Golden Stone. These can all be viewed as three levels of initiation and Rosenkreutz has to sign his name in a special book in each case, giving assurances and promises relating to the level he is at.

## The Characters

We come across 21 characters in all, 14 of which play only a minor role. The remaining seven are: *Christian Rosenkreutz*, the *First Porter*, the *Virgin*, the old *Queen* (Duchess), the *Bridegroom* (King), *Atlas* the court astronomer and counsellor and the *Warder* of the Tower of Olympus.

Essentially the relationship between Rosenkreutz and the Bridegroom or King is at the centre of this allegory since it is the disposition of the Bridegroom that represents the state of spiritual development to which the main character has attained. Actions taken by Rosenkreutz, therefore, ensure the eventual resurrection of the Bridegroom. This is confirmed on the seventh day where Rosenkreutz is referred to as "his father."

The Virgin appears from day three to six and seems to be the figure of authority in the Castle during this time. She guides events while the male characters remain in the background. There is much interplay between her and Rosenkreutz providing much of the action and entertainment. A clue to her role as the agent of events is given when Rosenkreutz plucks up enough courage to ask her name. She responds by giving him a riddle to solve in order to come by it. The answer is *Alchymia*, which is interesting when we consider that it is by the process of alchemical working (once one has achieved experience with the Book of Nature) that the inner processes are sublimated.

The First Porter appears at the beginning and end of the story. He and Rosenkreutz are connected in a way that is not apparent until the end. We then find out that this character has also observed in the past the sleeping Venus in the chamber beneath the Castle. It seems that those who live within the Castle are preoccupied with dry abstract science and religion, largely a male preserve, at the expense of losing this female element which is represented by the immured Venus. Given the general associations with this archetype perhaps we can carry the interpretation a little further and say that they lack *Love* which is the key ingredient for a perfected world. Those aware of this secret are qualified to take on the role of Guardian at the First Portal, as Rosenkreutz does at the end, since they can recognise those who are worthy enough to enter.

The characters of Old Atlas and the Warder of the Tower come into play on the seventh day. Atlas, who is also an astrologer, represents the realm of the Castle while the Warder represents the Tower. If Rosenkreutz is viewed as the initiate of the outer world, we have in these three personas a representation of the three levels in the allegory.

The old Queen, also known as the Duchess, is a most interesting character particularly in relation to the Virgin. She first appears near the end of the third day and is dressed so grandly that Rosenkreutz thinks at first that she is the Bride and she certainly gives the appearance of being richer, particularly as she also wears a coronet. Her entry is apart from the rest with her head turned "towards heaven." This initial entrance gives us a clue as to what she represents. This is confirmed later when we find that her room has prayer books and a pulpit from where she prays. Also, on the fourth day, while leading the procession to see the Comedy, she carries a crucifix made of pearl before her.

Clearly this figure represents religious authority or "Theologia" in contrast to the figure of the Virgin, "Alchymia." Rosenkreutz makes the distinction by telling the reader of her haughty tone which "pierced his bones and marrow" in contrast to that "of our Virgin, who was somewhat more worldly." There is a dichotomy here in that the Queen represents the feminine aspect immersed in heavenly devotion and world renunciation as opposed to the Virgin whose feminine impulse is toward spiritual fulfilment in the earthly realm. But to clarify further, we can say that Theology brings us to spiritual awareness by directing our gaze upwards and renouncing the world in contrast to Alchemy which concerns inner transformation and an embracing of the earthly realm.

## Inner Transformation

The events and happenings surrounding the progress of Christian Rosenkreutz within the Castle all have a common purpose, namely, to prepare, teach and transform his soul personality, but principally in spiritual alchemical terms, it is a directed working towards reintegration of his male and female aspects. This change in consciousness is well indicated by the way the dreams he has at the end of each day affect him. From the third day onward he is less concerned about the significance of his dreams and begins to have more spiritual insight from his conscious experiences.

On the fifth day when Rosenkreutz is sailing across the great lake in a fleet of seven ships, a host of sirens begin to sing to them. Their song emphasises the power of Love and its ability to unite opposites:

> *And as long as we live,*
> *God graciously give;*
> *That as great love and amity,*
> *They bear each other mightily;*
> *So we likewise, by Love's own flame,*
> *May reconjoyn them once again.*

The effect on Rosenkreutz at these words of Love causes him to be nearly overcome by giddiness or emotion. He understands the meaning of the siren's song and the transformative power Love has to bring the Bridegroom and Bride together as one.

# The Tower of Olympus

This is the third level of attainment where the process of transformation of Rosenkreutz and those eight other adepts accompanying him is further developed. Here they have to ascend seven levels where each level represents a further raising of consciousness and corresponding spiritual transformation. There are only three ways in which to achieve this: by the use of wings, ladders and ropes, each one representing the three paths of spiritual development. These are respectfully the mystical, the hermetic and the magical.

- ❖ At the *first* level the initiates have to do some practical alchemical work involving preparing essences of stones and plants.
- ❖ On the *second* there is a procession around a great vessel containing the bodies of the Kings and Queens, and they witness the distillation process upon the bodies using the essences of the Moor's head.
- ❖ Once they are admitted to the *third* level they observe the effect of sunlight by the use of mirrors to collectively increase its power upon the distilled bodies which are heated within a globe suspended from the ceiling. After this process the globe is opened and Rosenkreutz and his companions see that the substance has now changed into a great white egg.
- ❖ At the *fourth* level the egg is placed inside a square vessel made of copper upon which is inscribed some strange lettering. This is followed by the hatching of the egg into a Bird. It is fed three times by the "blood of the beheaded" from the executions on the previous fourth day, which causes it to grow quickly. Rosenkreutz observes that the Bird changes colour at each of the three feedings, from black to white to multi-coloured feathers. These correspond to the three alchemical stages of *nigredo* (depicted as a black crow in alchemical drawings), *albedo* (a white swan) and multi-coloured, usually depicted as a peacock's tail feathers.
- ❖ When they arrive at the *fifth* level the Bird is set into a bath of milky liquid that has been coloured so from a "fine white

powder." This is heated enough to remove the feathers and causing the water to take on a blue tinge. The Bird, which is now smooth, is removed and the liquid heated vigorously to evaporate it leaving a blue stone. This is taken out and pounded to produce a pigment with which they paint the Bird blue except for the head leaving it white.

❖ On the *sixth* level the altar we saw on the fourth day appears with its six ritual objects which include a *book*, an ever burning *taper*, a *sphere* or globe revolving by itself, a small striking *clock*, an ever flowing *fountain* and a *skull* with a serpent forever circling through the eye sockets. Excepting the book, they all display the property of eternal motion. The addition of the Bird makes seven objects in all. First it drinks from the fountain and then it pecks at the serpent making it bleed. The blood is gathered into a golden cup and then fed back to the Bird. They wait for the clock to strike two and for the conjunction indicated by the turning globe whereupon the Bird promptly lies it's head on the book and is beheaded by one of the initiates chosen previously by lot. They are affected by emotion at the death of the Bird but nevertheless assist the Virgin to incinerate the body to ash by using the taper.

At this point Rosenkreutz and three of his companions are tricked into believing that they have failed in their work and are led out of the door only to be congratulated on the other side. The remaining three alchemists have failed since they can only attain to the art of transmuting metals.

❖ And so the successful four are led to the *seventh* level; their work here is of the highest order. They have the task of resurrecting the King and Queen under the guidance of the Warder of the Tower. After performing this alchemical process the King and Queen are awakened by Cupid and they are dressed by the Virgin in garments of crystal. The royal couple then embark upon a ship and sail out of sight.

# Postscript

Given the difficult writing style of this early 17<sup>th</sup> century allegory, the modern reader really has to concentrate on the text. But this is perhaps useful in that it forces one's attention to the details, some of which are crucially important. Of course we can't pretend that just by reading the *Chymical Wedding* we will understand all of its contents without resorting to the use of a commentary of some sort.

While definitely not exhaustive it is to be hoped that this introduction, and part commentary, has gone some way toward making the narrative more interesting to read. In addition there are copious footnotes throughout the text that clarify some of the finer points.

1. The architecture here elaborated is based on that of Adam McLean in his *Commentary on the Chymical Wedding,* Magnum Opus Hermetic Sourceworks, 1984.

2. The significance and meaning of lettering such as this is explained in the footnotes as the reader progresses through the text.

# The Chemical Wedding of Christian Rosenkreutz

*An Hermetic Allegory*
*in Seven Parts*

*"Mysteries made public become cheap*
*and things profaned lose their grace."*

*"Therefore, cast not pearls before swine,*
*nor make a bed of roses for an ass."*

Being the

Third Manifesto

Anno 1616

# Chymische Hoch-
## zeit:
### Christiani Rosencreütz.
#### ANNO 1459.

*Arcana publicata vilescunt; & gra-*
*tiam prophanata amittunt.*

*Ergo: ne Margaritas obijce porcis, seu*
*Asino substerne rosas.*

**Straßburg,**
In Verlegung / Lazari Zetzners.
*Anno M. DC. XVI.*

*Title page of the Chymical Wedding in German, 1616.*

# The First Day

ON AN EVENING BEFORE EASTER-DAY, I sat at a table, and having (as my custom was) in my humble prayer sufficiently conversed with my Creator, and considered many great mysteries (whereof the Father of Lights his Majesty had shewn me not a few) and being now ready to prepare in my heart, together with my dear Paschal Lamb, a small, unleavened, undefiled cake; All on a sudden ariseth so horrible a tempest, that I imagined no other but that through its mighty force, the hill whereon my little house was founded, would flye in pieces.

But in as much as this, and the like from the Devil (who had done me many a spight) was no new thing to me, I took courage, and persisted in my meditation, till some body after an unusual manner, touched me on the back; whereupon I was so hugely terrified, that I durst hardly look about me; yet I shewed myself as cheerful as (in the like occurrence.) humane frailty would permit; now the same thing still twitching me several times. by the coat, I looked back, and behold it was a fair and glorious lady, whose garments were all skye-colour, and curiously (like Heaven) bespangled with golden stars, in her right hand she bare a trumpet of beaten gold, whereon a Name was ingraven which I could well read in but am as yet forbidden to reveal it. In her left hand she had a great bundle of letters of all languages, which she (as I afterwards understood) was to carry into all countries. She had also large and beautiful wings, full of eyes throughout, wherewith she could mount aloft, and flye swifter than any eagle.

I might perhaps been able to take further notice of her, but because she stayed so small time with me, and terror and amazement still possessed me, I was fain to be content. For as soon as I turned about, she turned her letters over and over, and at length drew out a small one, with which great reverence she laid down upon the table, and without giving one word, departed from me. But in her mounting upward, she gave so mighty a blast on her gallant trumpet, that the whole hill echoed thereof, and for a full quarter of an hour after, I could hardly hear my own words.

In so unlooked for an adventure I was at a loss, how either to advise, or assist my poor self, and therefore fell upon my knees and besought my Creator to permit nothing contrary to my eternal happiness to befall me; whereupon with fear and trembling, I went to the letter, which was now so heavy, as had it been mere gold, it could hardly have been so weighty. Now as I was diligently viewing it, I found a little seal, whereupon a curious cross with this inscription, IN HOC SIGNO VINCES,[1] was ingraven.

Now as soon as I espied this sign I was the more comforted, as not being ignorant that such a seal was little acceptable, and much less useful, to the Devil. Whereupon I tenderly opened the letter, and within it, in an azure field, in golden letters, found the following verses written.[2]

> *This day, this day, this, this*
> *The Royal Wedding is.*
> *Art thou thereto by birth inclin'd,*
> *And unto joy of God design'd,*
> *Then may'st thou to the mountain trend,*
> *Whereon three stately temples stand,*
> *And there see all from end to end.*
> *Keep watch, and ward,*
> *Thy self regard;*
> *Unless with diligence thou bathe,*
> *The Wedding can't thee harmless save;*
> *He'l damage have that here delays;*
> *Let him beware, too light that weighs.*

Underneath stood Sponsus and Sponsa.[3]

As soon as I had read this letter, I was presently like to have fainted away, all my hair stood on end, and a cold sweat trickled down my whole body. For although I well perceived that this was the appointed wedding, whereof seven years before I was acquainted

---

[1] "In this sign you will be victorius."
[2] This manifesto is the first English translation by E. Foxcroft (1690). He has attempted here to retain the rhyming pattern of the verses, producing a somewhat awkward English in the process.
[3] "Bride and Bridegroom."

in a bodily vision, and which now so long time I had with great earnestness attended, and which lastly, by the account and calculation of the planets, I had most diligently observed, I found so to be, yet could I never fore-see that it must happen under so grievous perilous conditions. For whereas I before imagined that to be a well-come and acceptable guest, I needed only be ready to appear at the wedding, I was now directed to Divine Providence, of which until this time I was never certain.

I also found by my self, the more I examined my self, that in my head there was nothing but gross misunderstanding, and blindness in mysterious things, so that I was not able to comprehend even those things which lay under my feet, and which I daily conversed with, much less that I should be born to the searching out, and understanding of the secrets of Nature, since in my opinion Nature might every where find a more virtuous disciple, to whom to intrust her precious, though temporary, and changeable treasures.

I found also that my bodily behaviour, and outward good conversation, and brotherly love toward my neighbour, was not duly purged and cleansed; moreover the tickling of the flesh manifested itself, whose affection was bent only to pomp and bravery, and worldly pride, and not to the good of mankind: and I was always contriving how by this art I might in a short time abundantly increase my profit and advantage, rear up stately palaces, make my self an everlasting name in the world, and other like carnal designs. But the obscure words concerning the three temples did particularly afflict me, which I was not able to make out by any after-speculation, and perhaps should not yet, had they not been wonderfully revealed to me.

Thus sticking betwixt hope and fear, examining my self again and again, and finding only my own frailty and impotency, not being in any wise able to succour myself, and exceedingly amazed at the fore-mentioned threatening, at length I betook myself to my usual and most secure course; after I had finished my earnest and most fervent prayer, I laid me down in my bed, that so perchance my good angel by the Divine permission might appear, and (as it had sometimes formerly happened) instruct me in this doubtful affair, which to the praise of God, my own good, and my neighbours faithful and hearty warning and amendment did now likewise fall out.

For I was yet scarce fallen asleep, when me-thought, I, together with a numberless multitude of men lay fettered with great chains in a dark dungeon, wherein without the least glimpse of light, we swarmed like bees one over another, and thus rendered each others affliction more grievous. But although neither I, nor any of the rest could see one jot, yet I continually heard one heaving himself above the other, when his chains or fetters were become ever so little lighter, though none of us had much reason to shove up the other, since we were all captive wretches.

Now as I with the rest had continued a good while in this affliction, and each was still reproaching the other with his blindness and captivity, at length we heard many trumpets sounding together, and kettle drums beating so artificially thereto, that it even revived and rejoiced us in our calamity. During this noise the cover of the dungeon was from above lifted up, and a little light let down unto us. Then first might truly have been discerned the bustle we kept, for all went pesle-mesle, and he who perchance had too much heaved up himself, was forced down again under the others feet. In brief, each one strove to be uppermost, neither did I my self linger, but with my weighty fetters slipt up from under the rest, and then heaved myself upon a stone, which I laid hold of; howbeit, I was several times caught at by others, from whom yet as well as I might, with hands and feet I still guarded my self. For we imagined no other but that we should all be set at liberty, which yet fell out quite otherwise.

For after the nobles who looked upon us from above through the hole, had a while recreated themselves with this our struggling and lamenting, a certain hoary-headed ancient man called us to be quiet, and having scarce obtained it, began (as I still remember) thus to say on.

> *If wretched mankind would forbear*
> *Themselves so to uphold,*
> *Then sure on them much good confer,*
> *My righteous Mother would:*
> *But since the same will not ensue,*
> *They must in care and sorrow rue,*
> *And still in prison lie.*

*Howbeit, my dear Mother will*
*Their follies over-see,*
*Her choicest goods permitting still*
*Too much in the light to be.*
*Though very rarely it may seem*
*That they may still keep some esteem,*
*Which else would pass for forgery.*

*Wherefore in honour of the feast*
*We this day solemnise,*
*That so her grace may be increast,*
*A good deed she'd devise.*
*For now a cord shall be let down,*
*And whosoe'er can hang thereon,*
*Shall freely be releast.*

He had scarce done speaking when an ancient matron commanded her servants to let down the cord seven times into the dungeon, and draw up whosoever could hang upon it. Good God! that I could sufficiently describe the hurry and disquiet that then arose amongst us for every one strove to get to the cord, and yet only hindered each other. But after seven minutes a sign was given by a little bell, whereupon at the first pull the servants drew up four. At that time I could not come near the cord by much, having (as is before-mentioned) to my huge misfortune, betaken my self to a stone at the wall of the dungeon, and thereby was disabled to get to the cord which descended in the middle.

The cord was let down the second time, but divers, because their chains were too heavy, and their hands too tender, could not keep their hold on the cord, but with themselves beat down many another, who else perhaps might have held fast enough; nay, many an one was forcibly pulled off by another, who yet could not himself get at it, so mutually envious were we even in this our great misery. But they of all others most moved my compassion, whose weight was so heavy, that they tore their very hands from their bodies, and yet could not get up. Thus it came to pass that at those five times very few were drawn up. For as soon as the sign was given, the servants were so nimble at the draught, that the most part tumbled one upon another, and the cord, this time especially, was drawn up very empty.

Whereupon the greatest part, and even I myself, despaired of redemption, and called upon God that he would have pity on us, and (if possible) deliver us out of this obscurity, who also then heard some of us: for when the cord came down the sixth time, some of them hung themselves fast upon it; and whilst in the drawing up, the cord swung from one side to the other, it (perhaps by the will of God) came to me, which I suddenly catching, uppermost above all the rest, and so at length beyond hope came out; whereat I exceedingly rejoiced, so that I perceived not the wound, which in the drawing up I received on my head by a sharp stone, till I with the rest who were released (as was always before done) was fain to help at the seventh and last pull, at which time through straining, the blood ran down all over my clothes, which I nevertheless for joy regarded not. Now when the last draught whereon the most of all hung, was finished, the matron caused the cord to be laid away, and willed her aged son to declare her resolution to the rest of the prisoners, who after he had a little bethought himself spoke, thus unto them.

> *Ye children dear*
> *All present here,*
> *What is but now complete and done,*
> *Was long before resolved on:*
> *What er'r my mother of great grace*
> *To each on both sides here hath shown,*
> *May never discontent mix-place;*
> *The joyful time is drawing on,*
> *When every one shall equal be,*
> *None wealthy, none in penury.*
> *Who er'e receiveth great commands*
> *Hath work enough to fill his hands.*
> *Who er'e with much hath trusted been,*
> *'Tis well if he may save his skin.*
> *Wherefore your lamentations cease,*
> *What is't to wait for some few days?*

As soon as he had finished these words, the cover was again put to and locked down, and the trumpets and kettle-drums began afresh, yet could not the noise thereof be so loud, but that the bitter lamentation of the prisoners which arose in the dungeon was heard above all, which soon also caused my eyes to run-over.

Presently after the ancient matron, together with her son sat down on seats before prepared, and commanded the redeemed should be told. Now as soon as she understood the number, and had written it down in a gold-yellow tablet, she demanded every ones name, which were also written down by a little page; having viewed us all, one after another, she sighed, and spoke to her son, so as I could well hear her, *"Ah how hartily am I grieved for the poor men in the dungeon! I would to God I durst release them all."*

Whereunto her son replied; *"It is mother thus ordained of God, against whom we may not contend. In case we all of us were lords, and possessed all the goods upon Earth, and were seated at table, who would there then be to bring up the service?"*

Whereupon his mother held her peace, but soon after she said; *"Well, however, let these be freed from their fetters,"* which was likewise presently done, and I, except a few was the last; yet I could not refrain, but (though I still looked upon the rest) bowed myself before the ancient matron, and thanked God that through her, had graciously and fatherly vouchsafed to bring me out of such darkness into the light: after me the rest did likewise, to the satisfaction of the matron.

Lastly, to every one was given a piece of gold for a remembrance, and to spend by the Way, on the one whereof was stamped the rising sun, on the other (as I remember) these three letters, D.L.S.,[1] and therewith every one had license to depart, and was sent to his own business with this annexed intimation, that we to the glory of God should benefit our neighbours, and reserve in silence what we had been intrusted with, which we also promised to do, and so departed one from another. But in regard of the wounds which the fetters had caused me, I could not well go forward, but halted on both feet, which the matron presently espying, laughing at it and calling me again to

---

[1] Abbreviation for *Deus Lux Solis*, or *Deo Laus Semper*. "God is the light of the Sun", or "God be praised for ever".

her said thus to me, *"My son, let not this defect afflict thee, but call to mind thy infirmities, and therewith thank God who hath permitted thee even in this world, and in the state of thy imperfection to come into so high a light, and keep these wounds for my sake."*

Whereupon the trumpets began again to sound, which so affrighted me that I awoke, and then first perceived that it was only a dream, which was so strongly impressed upon my imagination, that I was still perpetually troubled about it, and me thought I was yet sensible of the wounds on my feet. Howbeit, by all these things I well understood that God had vouchsafed that I should be present at this mysterious and bidden wedding; wherefore with childlike confidence I returned thanks to his Divine Majesty, and besought him, that he would further preserve me in his fear, that he would daily fill my heart with wisdom and understanding, and at length graciously (without my desert) conduct me to the desired end.

Hereupon I prepared my self for the way, put on my white linen coat, girded my loins, with a blood-red ribbon bound-cross-ways over my shoulder. In my hat I stuck four red roses, that I might the sooner by this token be taken notice of amongst the throng. For food I took bread, salt and water, which by the counsel of an understanding person I had at certain times used, not without profit, in the like occurrences. But before I parted from my cottage, I first in this my dress and wedding garment, fell down upon my knees, and besought God, that in case such a thing were, he would vouchsafe me a good issue. And thereupon in the presence of God I made a Vow, that if any thing through his grace should be revealed unto me, I would employ it neither to my own honour nor authority in the world, but to the spreading of his Name, and the service of my neighbour. And with this vow, and good hope I departed out of my cell with joy.

# The Second Day

IT WAS HARDLY GOT OUT OF MY CELL into a forest when me thought the whole heaven and all the elements had already trimmed themselves against[1] this wedding. For even the birds chanted more pleasantly then before, and the young fawns skipped so merrily, that they rejoiced my old heart, and moved me to sing: wherefore with a loud voice I thus began:

*With mirth thou pretty bird rejoice,*
*Thy Maker's praise in-tranced.*
*Lift up thy shrill and pleasant voice,*
*Thy God is high advanced.*
*Thy food before he did provide,*
*And gives it in a fitting side,*
*Therewith be thou sufficed.*
*Why should'st thou now unpleasant be,*
*Thy wrath against God venting?*
*That he a little bird made thee,*
*Thy silly head tormenting?*
*Because he made thee not a man,*
*O peace, he hath well thought thereon.*
*Therewith be thou sufficed.*
*What is't I'd have poor earthly worm,*
*By God (as'twere) inditing,*
*That I should thus 'gainst Heaven storm*
*To force great arts by fighting?*
*God will out-braved be by none,*
*Who's good for naught, may hence be gone,*
*O man b' herewith sufficed.*
*That he no Caesar hath thee fram'd,*
*To pine therefore 'tis needless*
*His name perhaps thou hadst defam'd*
*Whereof he was not heedless*
*Most clear and bright Gods eyes do shine,*

---

[1] Meaning "in preparation for."

*He pierces to thy heart within,*
*And cannot be deceived.*

This sang I now from the bottom of my heart throughout the whole forest, so that it resounded from all parts, and the hills repeated my last words, until at length I espied a curious green heath, wither I betook my self out of the forest. Upon this heath stood three lovely tall cedars, which by reason of their breadth afforded an excellent and desired shade, whereat I greatly rejoiced; for although I had not hitherto gone far, yet my earnest longing made me very faint, whereupon I hasted to the trees to rest a little under them, but as soon as I came somewhat higher, I espied a tablet fastened to one of them, on which (as afterwards I read) in curious letters the following words were written:

*"God save thee, stranger! If thou hast heard anything concerning the nuptials of the King, consider these words. By us doth the Bridegroom offer thee a choice between four ways, all of which, if thou dost not sink down in the way, can bring thee to his royal court. The first is short but dangerous, and one which will lead thee into rocky places, through which it will be scarcely possible to pass. The second is longer, and takes thee circuitously; it is plain and easy, if by the help of the Magnet, thou turnest neither to left nor right. The third is that truly royal way which through various pleasures and pageants of our King, affords thee a joyful journey; but this so far has scarcely been allotted to one in a thousand. By the fourth shall no man reach the place, because it is a consuming way, practicable only for incorruptible bodies. Choose now which thou wilt of the three, and persevere constantly therein, for know which soever thou shalt enter, that is the one destined for thee by immutable Fate, nor canst thou go back therein save at great peril to life. These are the things which we would have thee know, but, ho, beware! thou knowest not with how much danger thou cost commit thyself to this way, for if thou knowest thyself by the smallest fault to be obnoxious to the laws of our King, I beseech thee, while it is still possible, to return swiftly to thy house by the way thou camest."*

As soon as I had read this writing all my joy was near vanished again, and I who before sang merrily, began now inwardly to lament. For although I saw all the three ways before me, and understood that hence forward it was vouchsafed me, to make choice of one of them, yet it troubled me that in case I went the stony and rocky way, I might get a miserable and deadly fall, or taking the long one, I might wander out of it through by-ways, or be otherway's detained in the great journey. Neither durst I hope, that I amongst thousands should be the very one who should choose the royal way. I saw likewise the fourth before me, but it was so invironed with fire and exhalations, that I durst not (by much) draw near it, and therefore again and again considered, whether I should turn back, or take any of the ways before me. I well weighted my own unworthiness, but the dream still comforted me, that I was delivered out of the tower, and yet I durst not confidently rely upon a dream; whereupon I was so variously perplexed, that for very great weariness, hunger and thirst seized me.

Whereupon I presently drew out my bread, cut a slice of it, which a snow-white dove of whom I was not aware, sitting upon the tree, espied and therewith (perhaps according to her wonted manner) came down, and betook herself very familiarly with me, to whom I willingly imparted my food, which she received, and so with her prettiness did again a little refresh me. But as soon as her enemy a most black raven perceived it, he straight darted himself down upon the dove, and taking no notice of me, would needs force away the dove's meat, who could no otherwise guard her self but by flight; whereupon they both together flew towards the south, at which I was so hugely incensed and grieved, that without thinking what I did, I made hast after the filthy raven, and so against my will ran into one of the forementioned ways a whole fields length; and thus the raven being chased away, and the dove delivered, I then first observed what I had inconsiderately done, and that I was already entered into a way, from which under peril of great punishment I durst not retire. And though I had still herewith in some measure to comfort my self, yet that which was worst of all to me, was, that I had left my bag and bread at the tree, and could never retrieve them. For as soon as I turned my self about, a contrary wind was so strong against me, that it was ready to fell me. But if I went forward on my way, I perceived no hinderance at all. From whence I could easily conclude, that it would cost me my life, in case I should set my self against the wind, wherefore I patiently took up my cross, got up on my feet, and resolved, since so it must be, I would use my utmost endeavour to get to my journeys end before night.

Now although many apparent byways shewed themselves, yet I still proceeded with my compass, and would not budge one step from the Meridian Line; howbeit the way was oftentimes so rugged and unpassable, that I was in no little doubt of it. On this way I constantly thought upon the dove and raven, and yet could not search out the meaning until at length upon a high hill afar off I espied a stately portal, to which not regarding how far it was distant both from me and the way I was in, I hasted, because the sun had already hid himself under the hills, and I could elsewhere espy no abiding place, and this verily I ascribe only to God, who might well have permitted me to go forward in this way, and withheld my eyes that so I might have gazed beside this gate. To which I now made mighty haste, and reached it by so much daylight, as to take a very competent view of it.

Now it was an exceeding royal beautiful portal, whereon were carved a multitude of most noble figures and devices, every one of which (as I afterwards learned) had its peculiar signification. Above was fixed a pretty large tablet, with these words, *Procul hinc, procul ite profani,*[1] and other things more, that I was earnestly forbidden to relate.

Now as soon as I was come under the portal, there straight stepped forth one in a sky-coloured habit, whom I in friendly manner saluted, which though he thankfully returned, yet he instantly demanded of me my letter of invitation. O how glad was I that I had then brought it with me. For how easily might I have forgotten it (as it also chanced to others) as he himself told me' I quickly presented it, wherewith he was not only satisfied, but (at which I much wondered) shewed me abundance of respect, saying, Come in my brother, an acceptable guest you are to me; and withal intreated me not to with-hold my name from him. Now having replied, that I was a Brother of the Red-Rosie Cross, he both wondered, and seemed to rejoice at it, and then proceeded thus, My brother, have you nothing about you wherewith to purchase a token? I answered my ability was small, but if he saw any thing about me he had a mind to, it was at his service. Now he having requested of me my bottle of water, and I granted it he gives

---

[1] "Begone, begone, ye who are not called."

me a golden token whereon stood no more but these two letters, S. C.,[1] intreating me that when it stood me in good stead, I would remember him. After which I asked him, how many were got in before me, which he also told me, and lastly out of mere friendship gave me a sealed letter to the second Porter.

Now having lingered some time with him, the night grew on. Whereupon a great beacon upon the gates was immediately fired, that so if any were still upon the way, he might make hasted hither. But the way where it finished at the castle, was on both sides inclosed with walls, and planted with all sorts of excellent fruit trees, and still on every third tree on each side lanterns were hung up, wherein all the candles were already lighted with a glorious torch by a beautiful Virgin, habited in skye-colour, which was so noble and majestic a spectacle, that I yet delayed somewhat longer than was requisite. But at length after sufficient information, and an advantageous instruction, I friendly departed from the first Porter.

On the way, though I would gladly have known what was written in my letter, yet since I had no reason to mistrust the Porter, I forbare my purpose, and so went on the way, until I came likewise to the second gate, which though it was very like the other, yet was it adorned with images and mystic significations. In the affixed tablet stood *Date et dabitur vobis*.[2] Under this gate lay a terrible grim lion chain'd, who as soon as he espied me arose and made at me with great roaring; whereupon the second Porter who lay upon a stone of marble awaked, and wished me not to be troubled or affrighted, and then drove back the lion, and having received the letter which I with trembling reached him, he read it, and with very great respect spake thus to me, *"Now well-come in Gods Name unto me the man whom of long time I would gladly have seen."* Meanwhile he also drew out a token, and asked me whether I could purchase it? But having nothing else left but my salt, presented it to him, which he thankfully accepted. Upon this token again stood only two letters, namely, S. M.[3]

---

[1] Abreviation for *Santitate Constantia, Sponsus Charus, Spes Charias.* "Steadfastness in piety. Well beloved bridegroom, hope and love."

[2] "Give and it will be given to you."

[3] Abbreviation for *Studio Merentis, Sal Humor Sponso Mittendus, Sal Mineralis, Sal Menstrualis.* "To the worthy in study, pawn of the bridegroom, mineral salt, salt of purification."

Being now just about to enter discourse with him, it began to ring in the castle, whereupon the Porter counselled me to run apace, or else all the pains and labour I had hitherto taken would serve to no purpose, for the lights above began already to be extinguished; whereupon I dispatched with such haste that I heeded not the Porter, in such anguish was I, and truly it was but necessary, for I could not run so fast but that the Virgin, after whom all the lights were put out, was at my heels, and I should never have found the way, had not she with her torch afforded me some light; I was moreover constrained to enter the very next to her, and the gate was so suddenly clap's to, that a part of my coat was locked out, which I was verily forced to leave behind me; for neither I, nor they who stood ready without and called at the gate could prevail with the Porter to open it again, but he delivered the keys to the Virgin, who took them with her into the court.

Mean time I again surveyed the gate, which now appeared so rich, as the whole world could not equal it; just by the door were two columns on one of which stood a pleasant figure with this inscription, *Congratulor*. The other having its countenance veiled was sad, and beneath was written, *Condoleo*.[1] In brief, the inscriptions and figures thereon, were so dark and mysterious, that the most dexterous man upon earth could not have expounded them. But all these (if God permit) I shall ever long publish and explain.

Under this gate I was again to give my name, which was this last time written down in a little vellum book, and immediately with the rest dispatched to the Lord Bridegroom. Here it was where I first received the true guest token, which was somewhat less than the former, but yet much heavier. Upon this stood these letters, S. P. N.[2] Besides this, a new pair of shoes were given me, for the floor of the castle was laid with pure shining marble; my old shoes I was to give away to one of the poor who sate in throngs, howbeit in very good order, under the gate. I then bestowed them on an old man; after which two pages with as many torches conducted me into a little room.

---

[1] Meaning "to congratulate" and "I condole."

[2] *Sponsi praesentandus nuptiis. Salus per naturam*; which means "to be presented at the bridegroom's nuptials. Salvation through Nature."

There they willed me to sit down on a form, which I did, but they sticking their torches in two holes, made in the pavement, departed and thus left me sitting alone. Soon after I heard a noise, but saw nothing, and it proved to be certain men who stumbled in upon me; but since I could see nothing, I was fain to suffer, and attend what they would do with me; but presently perceiving them to be barbers, I intreated them not to jostle me so, for I was content to do whatever they desired, whereupon they quickly let me go, and so one of them (whom I could not yet see) fine and gently cut away the hair-round about from the crown of my head, but on my forehead, ears and eyes he permitted my ice-grey locks to hang. In his first encounter (I must confess) I was ready to dispair, for inasmuch as some of them shoved me so forceably, and I could yet see nothing, I could think no other but that God for my curiosity had suffered me to miscarry. Now these invisible barbers carefully gathered up the hair which was cut off, and carried it away with them.

After which the two pages entered again, and heartily laughed at me for being so terrified. But they had scarce spoken a few words with me, when again a little bell began to ring, which (as the pages informed me) was to give notice for assembling; whereupon they willed me to rise, and through many walks, doors and winding stairs lighted me into a spacious hall. In this room was a great multitude of guests, emperors, kings, princes, and lords, noble and ignoble, rich and poor, and all sorts of people, at which I hugely marvelled, and thought to my self, ah, how gross a fool hast thou been to engage upon this journey with so much bitterness and toil, when (behold) here are even those fellows whom thou well know'st, and yet hadst never any reason to esteem. They are now all here, and thou with all thy prayers and supplications art hardly got in at last. This and more the Devil at that time injected, whom I notwithstanding (as well as I could) directed to the issue.

Mean time one or other of my acquaintance here and there spoke to me: "*Oh Brother Rosencreutz! Art thou here too?*"

"*Yea, (my brethren),*" replied I, "*the grace of God hath helped me in also.*"

At which they raised a mighty laughter, looking upon it as ridiculous that there should be need of God in so slight an occasion.

Now having demanded each of them concerning his way, and found that most were forced to clamber over the rocks, certain trumpets (none of which we yet saw) began to sound to the table, whereupon they all seated themselves, every one as he judged himself above the rest; so that for me and some other sorry fellows there was hardly a little nook left at the lower-most table.

Presently the two pages entered, and one of them said grace in so handsom and excellent manner, as rejoyced the very heart in my body. Howbeit, certain great St John's made but little reckoning of them, but fleired and winked one at another, biting their lips within their hats, and using more the like unseemly gestures. After this, meat was brought in, and albeit none could be seen, yet every thing was so orderly managed, that it seemed to me as if every guest had had his proper attendant. Now my artists having somewhat recruited themselves, and the wine having a little removed shame from their hearts, they presently began to vaunt and brag of their abilities. One would prove this, another that, and commonly the most sorry idiots made the loudest noise. Ah, when I call to mind what preternatural and impossible enterprises I then heard, I am still ready to vomit at it. In fine, they never kept in their order, but when ever one rascal here, another there, could insinuate himself in between the nobles; then pretended they the finishing of such adventures as neither Sampson, nor yet Hercules with all their strength could ever have achieved: this would discharge Atlas of his burden; the other would again draw forth the three-headed Cerberus out of Hell. In brief, every man had his own prate, and yet the great lords were so simple that they believed their pretences, and the rogues so audacious, that although one or other of them was here and there rapped over the fingers with a knife, yet they flinched not at it, but when any one perchance had filched a gold-chain, then would all hazard for the like.

I saw one who heard the rustling of the heavens. The second could see Plato's ideas. A third could number Democritus' atoms. There were also not a few pretenders to the perpetual motion. Many an one (in my opinion) had good understanding, but assumed too much to himself, to his own destruction Lastly, there was one also who would needs out of hand persuade us that he saw the servitors who attended, and would still have pursued his contention, had not one of those invisible waiters reached him so handsom a cuff upon his lying muzzle, that not only he, but many more who were by him, became as mute as mice.

But it best of all pleased me, that all those, of whom I had any esteem, were very quiet in their business, and made no loud cry of it, but acknowledged themselves to be misunderstanding men, to whom the mysteries of nature were too high, and they themselves much too small. In this tumult I had almost cursed the day wherein I came hither; for I could not but with anguish behold that those lewd vain people were above at the board, but I in so sorry a place could not rest in quiet, one of those rascals scornfully reproaching me for a motley fool.

Now I thought not that there was yet one gate behind, through which we must pass, but imagined I was during the whole wedding, to continue in this scorn, contempt and indignity, which yet I had at no time deserved, either of the Lord Bridegroom or the Bride. And therefore (in my opinion) he should have done well to sort out some other fool to his wedding than me. Behold, to such impatience cloth the iniquity of this world reduce simple hearts. But this really was one part of my lameness, whereof (as is before mentioned) I dreamed. And truly this clamour the longer it lasted, the more it increased. For there were already those who boasted of false and imaginary visions, and would persuade us of palpably lying dreams.

Now there sat by me a very fine quiet man, who oftentimes discoursed of excellent matters. At length he said, "*Behold my brother, if any one should now come who were willing to instruct these blockish people in the right way, would he be heard?*"

"*No, verily,*" replied I.

"*The world*" said he, "*is now resolved (whatever comes on it) to be cheated, and cannot abide to give ear to those who intend its good. Seest thou also that same cocks-comb, with what whimsical figures and foolish conceits he allures others to him. There one makes mouthes at the people with the unheard-of mysterious words. Yet believe me in this, the time is now coming when those shameful vizards shall be plucked off, and all the world shall know what vagabond imposters were concealed behind them. Then perhaps that will be valued which at present is not esteemed.*"

Whilst he was thus speaking, and the clamour the longer it

lasted the worse it was, all on a sudden there began in the hall such excellent and stately musick, as all the days of my life I never heard the like; whereupon every one held his peace, and attended what would become of it. Now there were in this music all sorts of stringed instruments imaginable, which sounded together in such harmony, that I forgot myself, and sat so unmovable, that those who sat by me were amazed at me, and this lasted near half an hour, wherein none of us spoke one word. For as soon as ever any one was about to open his mouth, he got an unexpected blow, neither knew he from whence it came. Me thought since we were not permitted to see the musicians, I should have been glad to view only all the instruments they made use of. After half an hour this music ceased unexpectedly, and we could neither see nor hear any thing further.

Presently after, before the door of the hall began a great noise sounding and beating of trumpets, shalms and kettle-drums, also master-like, as if the Emperor of Rome had been entering; whereupon the door opened of itself, and then the noise of the trumpets was so loud, that we were hardly able to indure it. Meanwhile (to my thinking) many thousand small tapers came into the hall, all which of themselves marched in so very exact an order as altogether amazed us, till at last the two aforementioned pages with bright torches, lighting in a most beautiful Virgin, all drawn on a gloriously gilded triumphant self-moving throne, entered the hall. It seemed to me she was the very same who before on the way kindled, and put out the lights, and that these her attendants were the very same whom she formerly placed at the trees. She was not now as before in skye-colour, but arrayed in a snow-white glittering robe, which sparkled of pure gold, and cast such a lustre that we durst not steadily behold it. Both the pages were after the same manner habited (albeit somewhat more slightly). As soon as they were come into the middle of the hall, and were descended from the throne, all the small tapers made obeisance before her. Whereupon we all stood up from our benches, yet every one staid in his own place. Now she having to us, and we again to her, shewed all respect and reverence, in a most pleasant tone she began thus to speak;

*The King my Lord most gracious,*
*Who now's not very far from us,*
*As also his most lovely Bride,*
*To him in troth and honour ti'd;*
*Already, with great joy indu'd,*
*Have your arrival hither view'd;*
*And do to every one,*
*and all Promise their grace in special;*
*And from their very hearts desire,*
*You may it at the same acquire;*
*That so their future nuptial joy*
*May mixed be with none's annoy.*

Hereupon with all her small tapers she again courteously bowed, and
presently after began thus:

*In the invitation writ, you know*
*That no man called was hereto*
*Who of God's rarest gifts good store*
*Had not received long before,*
*Adorned with all requisit's,*
*As in such cases it befit's.*
*How though they cannot well conceit*
*That any man's so desperate,*
*Under conditions so hard,*
*Here to intrude without regard;*
*Unless he have been first of all,*
*Prepared for this nuptial;*
*And therefore in good hopes do dwell*
*That with all you it will be well.*
*Yet men are grown so bold, and rude,*
*Not weighing their inepitude,*
*As still to thrust themselves in place*
*Whereto none of them called was.*
*No cocks-comb here himself may sell,*
*No rascal in with others steal;*
*For they resolve without all let*

*A wedding pure to celebrate.*
*So then the artists for to weighs*
*eals shall be fix'd the ensuing day;*
*Whereby each one may lightly find*
*What he hath left at home behind.*
*If here be any of that rout*
*Who have good cause themselves to doubt,*
*Let him seek quickly hence aside;*
*For that in ease he longer bide,*
*Of grace forelor'n, and quite undone*
*Betimes he must the gauntlet run.*
*If any now his conscience gall,*
*He shall tonight be left in th' hall*
*And be again releas't by morn,*
*Yet so he hither ne'er return.*
*If any man have confidence,*
*He with his waiter may go hence,*
*Who shall him to his chamber light*
*Where he may rest in peace tonight;*
*And there with praise await the scale*
*Or else his sleep may chance to fail.*
*The others here may take it well,*
*For who aim's 'bove what's possible,*
*'Twere better much he hence had pas't,*
*But of you all wee'l hope the best.*

As soon as she had done speaking this, she again made reverence, and sprung cheerfully into her throne, after which the trumpets began again to sound, which yet was not of force to take from many their grievous sighs. So they again conducted her invisibly away, but the most part of the small tapers remained in the room, and still one of them accompanied each of us.

In such perturbation 'tis not well possible to express what pensive thoughts and gestures were amongst us. Yet the most part were resolved to await the scale, and in ease things sorted not well, to depart (as they hoped) in peace. I had soon cast up my reckoning, and being my conscience convinced me of all ignorance, and unworthiness,

I purposed to stay with the rest in the hall, and chose much rather to content myself with the meal I had already taken, than to run the risk of a future repulse. Now after that every one by his small taper had severally been conducted into a chamber (each as I since understood into a peculiar one), there stayed nine of us, and amongst the rest he also, who discoursed with me at the table. But although our small tapers left us not, yet soon after within an hours time one of the aforementioned pages came in, and bringing a great bundle of cords with him, first demanded of us whether we had concluded to stay there, which when we had with sighs affirmed, he bound each of us in a several place, and so went away with our small tapers, and left us poor wretches in darkness.

Then some first began to perceive the imminent danger, and I my self could not refrain tears. For although we were not forbidden to speak, yet anguish and affliction suffered none of us to utter one word. For the cords were so wonderfully made, yet none could cut them, much less get them off his feet. Yet this comforted me, that still the future gain, of many an one, who had now betaken himself to rest, would prove very little to his satisfaction. But we by only one nights penance might expiate all our presumption; till at length in my sorrowful thoughts I fell asleep, during which I had a dream. Now although there be no great matter in it, yet I esteem it not impertinent to recount it.

Me thought I was upon an high mountain, and saw before me a great and large valley. In this valley were gathered together an unspeakable multitude of people, each of which had at his head a thread, by which he was hanged up towards Heaven, now one hung high, another low, some stood even quite upon the earth. But in the air there flew up and down an ancient man, who had in his hand a pair of sheers, wherewith here he cut one's, and there another's thread. Now he that was nigh the earth was so much the readier, and fell without noise, but when it happened to one of the high ones, he fell, so that the earth quaked. To some it came to pass that their thread was no stretched, that they came to the earth before the thread was cut. I took pleasure in this tumbling, and it joyed me at the heart, when he who had over-exalted himself in the air, of his wedding, got so shameful a fall, that it carried even some of his neighbours along with him. In like manner it also rejoiced me, that he who had all this while kept himself near the earth, could come down so fine and gently, that even his next men perceived it not.

But being now in my highest fit of jolity, I was unawares jogged by one of my fellow captives, upon which I was awaked, and was very much discontented with him. Howbeit, I considered my dream, and recounted it to my brother, who lay by me on the other side, who was not dissatisfied with it, but hoped some comfort might thereby be pretended. In such discourse we spent the remaining part of the night, and with longing expected the day.

# The Third Day

NOW AS SOON AS THE LOVELY DAY was broken, and the bright sun, having raised himself above the hills, had again betaken himself, in the high heaven, to his appointed office, my good champions began to rise out of their beds, and leisurely to make themselves ready unto the inquisition. Whereupon, one after another, they came again into the hall, and giving us a good morrow, demanded how we had slept; and having espied our bonds, there were some that reproved us for being so cowardly, and that we had not, as they, hazarded upon all adventures. Howbeit, same of them whose hearts still smote them made no loud cry of the business. We excused ourselves with our ignorance, hoping we should now be set at liberty, and learn wit by this disgrace, that they on the contrary had not yet altogether escaped, and perhaps their greatest danger was still to be expected.

At length each one being assembled, the trumpets began now again to sound and the kettle drums to beat as formerly, and we then imagined no other but that the Bridegroom was ready to present himself; which nevertheless was a huge mistake. For it was again the yesterday's Virgin who had arrayed her self all in red velvet, and girded her self with a white scarfe. Upon her head she had a green wreath of laurel, which hugely became her. Her train was now no more of small tapers, but consisted of two hundred men in harness, who were all (like her) cloathed in red and white.

Now as soon as they were alighted from the throne, she comes straight to us prisoners, and after she had saluted us, she said in few words, *"That some of you have been sensible of your wretched condition is hugely pleasing to my most mighty Lord, and he is also resolved you shall fare the better for it."*

And having espied me in my habit, she laughed and spake, *"Good lack! hast thou also submitted thy self to the yoke, I imagined thou wouldst have made thy self very smug,"* with which words she caused my eyes to run over. After which she commanded we should be unbound, and coupled together and placed in a station where we might well behold the scales. *"For,"* said she, *"it may yet fare better with them, than the presumptuous, who yet stand here at liberty."*

Mean time the scales which were intirely of gold were hung up in the midst of the hall. There was also a little table covered with red velvet, and seven weights placed thereon. First of all stood a pretty great one, next four little ones; lastly, two great ones severally. And these weights in proportion to their bulk were so heavy, that no man can believe or comprehend it. But each of the harnessed men had together with a naked sword a strong rope. These she distributed according to the number; of weights into seven bands and out of every band chose one for their proper weight; and then again sprung up into her high throne. Now as soon as she had made her reverence, with a very shrill tone she began thus to speak:

> *Who int' a painters room does go*
> *And nothing does of painting know,*
> *Yet does in prating thereof, pride it;*
> *Shall be of all the world derided.*
> *Who into th' artists order goes,*
> *And "hereunto was never chose;*
> *Yet with pretence of skill does pride it;*
> *Shall be of all the world derided.*
> *Who at a wedding does appear,*
> *And yet was ner'e intended there;*
> *Yet does in coming highly pride it;*
> *Shall be of all the world derided.*
> *Who now into this scale ascends,*
> *The weights not proving his fast friends,*
> *And that it bounces so does ride it;*
> *Shall be of all the world derided.*

As soon as the Virgin had done speaking, one of the Pages commanded each one to place himself according to his order, and one after another to step in: which one of the emperors made no scruple of, but first of all bowed himself a little towards the Virgin, and afterwards in all his stately attire went up: whereupon each captain laid in his weight; which (to the wonder of all) he stood out. But the last was too heavy for him, so that forth he must, and that with much anguish that (as it seemed to me) the Virgin her self had pity on him, who also beckoned to her people to hold their peace, yet was the good emperor bound and delivered over to the sixth band. Next him again came forth another emperor, who steps hautily into the scale, and having a great thick book under his gown, he imagined not to fail. But being scarce able to abide the third weight, and being unmercifully flung down, and his book in that affrightment flipping from him, all the soldiers began to laugh, and he was delivered up bound to the third band. Thus it went also with some others of the emperors who were all shamefully laughed at and captived.

After these comes forth a little short man with a curled brown beard, an emperor too, who after the usual reverence got up also, and held out so steadfastly, that me thought, and there been more weights ready, he would have outstood them; to whom the Virgin immediately arose, and bowed before him, causing him to put on a gown of red velvet, and at last reached him a branch of laurel, having good store of them upon her throne, upon the steps whereof she willed him to sit down. Now how, after him it fared with the rest of the emperors, kings and lords, would be too long to recount; but I cannot leave unmentioned that few of those great personages held out. Howbeit sundry eminent virtues (beyond my hopes) were found in many. One could stand out this, the second another, some two, some three, four or five, but few could attain to the just perfection; but everyone who failed, was miserably laughed at by the bands.

After the Inquisition had also passed over the gentry, the learned, and unlearned, and the rest, and in each condition perhaps one, it may be, two, but for the most part none, was found perfect, it came at length to those honest gentlemen the vagabond cheaters, and rascally *Lapidem Spitalanficum* makers, who were set upon the scale with such scorn, that I my self for all my grief was ready to burst my belly with laughing, neither could the very prisoners themselves refrain. For the most part could not abide that severe trial, but with whips and scourges were jerked out of the scale, and led to the other prisoners, yet to a suitable band. Thus of so great a throng so few remained, that I am ashamed to discover their number. Howbeit there were persons of quality also amongst them, who notwithstanding were (like the rest) honoured with velvet robes and wreaths of laurel.

The Inquisition being completely finished, and none but we poor coupled hounds standing aside, at length one of the captains stepped forth, and said, "*Gratious Madam, if it please your ladyship let these poor men, who acknowledged their misunderstanding, be set upon the scale also without their incurring any danger of penalty, and only for recreation's sake, if perchance any thing that is right may be found amongst them.*"

In the first place I was in great perplexity, for in my anguish this was my only comfort, that I was not to stand in such ignominy, or to be lashed out of the scale. For I nothing doubted but that many of the prisoners wished that they had stay'd ten nights with us in the hall. Yet since the Virgin consented, so it must be, and we being untied were one after another set up. Now although the most part miscarried, yet they were neither laughed at, nor scourged, but peaceably placed on one side. My companion was the fifth, who held out bravely, whereupon all, but especially the captain who made the request for us, applauded him, and the Virgin shewed him the usual respect. After him again two more were dispatched in an instant. But I was the eighth.

Now as soon as (with trembling) I stepped up, my companion who already sat by in his velvet, looked friendly upon me, and the Virgin her self smiled a little. But for as much as I out-stayed all the weights, the Virgin commanded them to draw me up by force, wherefore three men moreover hung on the other side of the beam, and yet could nothing prevail. Whereupon one of the Pages immediately stood up, and cried out exceeding loud, THAT IS HE. Upon which the other replied, Then let him gain his liberty, which the Virgin accorded; and being received with due ceremonies, the choice was given me to release one of the captives, whosoever I pleased; whereupon I made no long deliberation, but elected the first emperor whom I had long pittied, who was immediately set free, and with all respect seated amongst us.

Now the last being set up, and the weights proving too heavy for him, in the mean while the Virgin espied my roses, which I had taken out of my hat into my hands, and thereupon presently by her Page graciously requested them of me, which I readily sent her.

And so this first act was finished about ten in the fore-noon. Whereupon the trumpets began to sound again, which nevertheless we could not as yet see. Mean time the bands were to step aside with their prisoners, and expect the judgement. After which a council of the seven captains and us was set, and the business was propounded by the Virgin as president, who desired each one to give his opinion, how the prisoners were to be dealt with. The first opinion was that they should all be put to death, yet one more severely than another: namely those who had presumptuously intruded themselves contrary to the express conditions; others would have them kept close prisoners. Both which pleased neither the president nor me. At length by one of the emperors (the same whom I had freed) my companion, and my self the affair was brought to this point; that first of all the principal lords should with a befitting respect be led out of the castle; others might be carried out somewhat more scornfully. These would be stripped and caused to run out naked. The fourth with rods, whips or dogs, should be hunted out. Those who the day before willingly surrendered themselves, might be suffered to depart without any blame. And last of all those presumptuous ones, and they who behaved themselves so unseemly at dinner the day before, should be punished in body and life according to each man's demerit. This opinion pleased the Virgin well, and obtained the upper hand. There was moreover another dinner vouchsafed them, which they were soon acquainted with. But the execution was deferred till twelve at noon.

Herewith the Senate arose, and the Virgin also, together with her attendants returned to her usual quarter. But the uppermost table in the room was allotted to us, they requesting us to take it in good part till the business were fully dispatched. And then we should be conducted to the Lord Bridegroom and the Bride, with which we were at present well content. Mean time the prisoners were again brought into the hall, and each man seated according to his quality; they were likewise enjoined to behave themselves somewhat more civilly than they had done the day before, which yet they needed not to have been admonished, for without this, they had already put up their pipes.

And this I can boldly say, not with flattery, but in the love of truth, that commonly those persons who were of the highest rank, best understood how to behave themselves in so unexpected a misfortune. Their treatment was but indifferent, yet with respect, neither could they yet see their attendants, but to us they were visible, whereat I was exceeding joyful. Now although fortune had exalted us, yet we took not upon us more than the rest, advising them to be of good cheer, the event would not be so ill. Now although they would gladly have understood the sentence of us, yet we were so deeply obliged that none durst open his mouth about it.

Nevertheless we comforted them as well we could, drinking with them to try if the wine might make them any thing cheerfuller. Our table was covered with red velvet, beset with drinking cups of pure silver and gold, which the rest could not behold without amazement and very great anguish. But e'er we had seated ourselves, in came the two Pages, presenting every one in the Bride-groom's behalf, the Golden Fleece with a flying lion, requesting us to wear them at the table, and as became us to observe the reputation and dignity of the order, which his majesty had now vouchsafed us, and should suddenly be ratified with suitable ceremony. This we received with profoundest submission, promising obediently to perform whatsoever his Majesty should please. Besides these, the noble Page had a schedule, wherein we were set down in order. And for my part I should not otherwise be desirous to conceal my place, if perchance it might not be interpreted to pride in me, which yet is expressly against the fourth weight.

Now because our entertainment was exceedingly stately, we demanded one of the Pages, whether we might not have leave to send some choice bit to our friends and acquaintance, who making no difficulty of it, every one sent plentifully to his acquaintance by the waiters, howbeit they saw none of them; and forasmuch as they knew not whence it came, I we. my self desirous to carry somewhat to one of them, but as soon as I was risen, one of the waiters was presently at my elbow, saying he desired me to take friendly warning, for in case one of the Pages had seen it, it would have come to the King's ear, who would certainly have taken it amiss of me; but since none had observed it but himself, he purposed not to betray me, but that I ought for the time to come to have better regard to the dignity of the order. With which words the servant did really so astonish me, that for a long time after I scarce moved upon my seat, yet I returned him thanks for his faithful warning, as well as in haste and affright I was able.

Soon after the drums began to beat again, to which we were already accustomed: for we well knew it was the Virgin, wherefore we prepared ourselves to receive her, who was now coming in with her usual train, upon her high seat, one of the Pages bearing before her a very tall goblet of gold, and the other a patent in parchment. Being now after a marvellous artificial manner alighted from the seat, she takes the goblet from the Page, and presents the same in the King's behalf, saying, that it was brought from his Majesty, and that in honour of him we should cause it to go round. Upon the cover of this goblet stood Fortune curiously cast in gold, who had in her hand a red flying ensign, for which cause I drunk somewhat the more sadly, as having been but too well acquainted with Fortune's way-wardness. But the Virgin as well as we, was adorned with the Golden Fleece and lion, whence I observed, that perhaps she wan the president of the order. Wherefore we demanded of her how the order might be named? She answered that it was not yet seasonable to discover it, till the affair with the prisoners were dispatched. And therefore their eyes were still held, and what had hitherto happened to us, was to them only for an offence and scandal, although it were to be accounted as nothing, in regard of the honour that attended us. Hereupon she began to distinguish the patent which the other Page held into two different parts, out of which about thus much was read before the first company.

That they should confess that they had too lightly given credit to fictitious books, had assumed too much to themselves, and so came into this castle, albeit they were never invited into it, and perhaps the most part had presented themselves with design to make their market here, and afterwards to live in the greater pride and lordliness; and thus one had seduced another, and plunged him into this disgrace and ignominy, wherefore they were deservedly to be soundly punished. Which they with great humility readily acknowledged, and gave their hands upon it. After which a severe check was given to the rest, much to this purpose.

*"That they very well knew, and were in their consciences convinced, that they had forged false fictitious books, had befooled others, and cheated them, and thereby had diminished regal dignity amongst all. They knew in like manner what ungodly deceitful figures they had made use of, in so much a. they spared not even the Divine Trinity. but accustomed themselves to cheat people the country over. It was also now as clear as day with what practices they had endeavoured to ensnare the true guests, and introduce the ignorant: in like manner, that it was manifest to all the world, that they*

*wallowed in open whoredom, adultery, gluttony, and other uncleannesses. All which was against the express orders of our kingdom. In brief, they knew they had disparaged kingly majesty, even amongst the common sort, and therefore they should confess themselves to be manifest convicted vagabond-cheaters, knaves and rascals, whereby they deserved to be cashiered from the company of civil people, and severely to be punished."*

The good artists were loath to come to this confession, but inasmuch as not only the Virgin her self threatened, and swore their death, but the other party also vehemently raged at them, and unanimously cryed out, that they had most wickedly seduced them out of the Light, they at length, to prevent a huge misfortune, confessed the same with dolour, and yet withal alledged that what had herein happened was not to be animadverted upon them in the worst sense. For in as much as the lords were absolutely resolved to get into the castle, and had promised great sums of money to that effect, each one had used all craft to seize upon something, and so things were brought to that pass, as was now manifest before their eyes. But that it succeeded not, they in their opinion had deserved no more than the lords themselves; as who should have had so much understanding as to consider that in case any one had been sure of getting in, he would not, in so great peril, for the sake of a slight gain, have clambered over the wall with them.

Their books also sold so mightily, that whoever had no other mean to maintain himself, was fain to engage in such a cousenage. They hoped moreover, that if a right judgment were made, they should be found no way to have miscarried, as having behaved themselves towards the lords, as became servants, upon their earnest entreaty.

But answer was made them, that his Royal Majesty had determined to punish all, and every man, albeit one more severely than another. For although what had been alledged by them was partly true, and therefore the lords should not wholly be indulged, yet they had good reason to prepare themselves for death, who had so presumptuously obtruded themselves, and perhaps seduced the more ignorant against their will; as likewise they who with false books had violated royal majesty, as the same might be evinced out of their very writings and books.

Hereupon many began most pitteously to lament, cry, weep,

entreat, and prostrate themselves, all which notwithstanding could avail them nothing, and I much marvelled how the Virgin could be so resolute, when yet their misery caused our eyes to run over, and moved our compassion (although the most part of them had procured us much trouble, and vexation). For she presently dispatched her Page, who brought with him all the curiassiers which had this day been appointed at the scales, who were commanded each of them to take his own to him, and in an orderly procession, so as still each curiassier should go with one of the prisoners, to conduct them into her great garden. At which time each one so exactly recognised his own man, that I marvelled at it. Leave also was likewise given to my yesterday companions to go out into the garden unbound, and to be present at the execution of the sentence. Now as soon as every man was come forth, the Virgin mounted up into her high throne, requesting us to sit down upon the steps, and to appear at the judgment, which we refused not, but left all standing upon the table (except the goblet, which the Virgin committed to the Pages keeping) and went forth in our robes upon the throne, which of it self moved so gently as if we had passed in the air, till in this manner we came into the garden, where we arose altogether.

This garden was not extraordinary curious, only it pleased me that the trees were planted in so good order. Besides there ran in it a most costly fountain, adorned with wonderful figures and inscriptions, and strange characters (which God willing I shall mention in a future book). In this garden was raised a wooden scaffold, hung about with curiously painted figured coverlets. Now there were four galleries made one over another, the first more glorious than any of the rest, and therefore covered with a white taffeta curtain, so that at that time we could not perceive who-was behind it. The second was empty and uncovered. Again the two last were covered with red and blew taffeta. Now as noon as we were come to the scaffold, the Virgin bowed her self down to the ground, at which we were mightily terrified: for we might easily guess that the King and Queen must not be far off. Now we also having duely performed our reverence, the Virgin lead us up by the winding stairs into the second gallery, where she placed herself uppermost, and us in our former order. But how the emperor whom I had released, behaved himself towards me, both at this time as also before at the table, I cannot, without slander of wicked tongues, well relate. For he might well imagine in what anguish and sollicitude he now should have been, in case he were at present to attend the judgment with such ignominies and that only through me he hast not attained such dignity and worthiness.

Mean time the virgin who first of all brought me the invitation, and whom hitherto I had never since seen, stepped in. First she gave one blast upon her trumpet, and then with a very loud voice declared the sentence in this manner:

*"The Kings Majesty my most gratious Lord could from his heart wish, that all and every one here assembled, held upon his Majesty's invitation presented themselves so qualified, as that they might (to his honour) with greatest frequently have adorned this his appointed nuptial and joyful feast. But since it hath otherwise pleased Almighty God, his Majesty hath not whereat to murmur, but must be forced, contrary to his own inclination, to abide by the ancient and laudable constitutions of this Kingdom. But now, that his Majesty's innate clemency may be celebrated over all the world, he hath thus far absolutely dealt with his council and estates, that the usual sentence shall be considerably lenified.*

*"So that in the first place he in willing to vouchsafe to the lords and potentates, not only their lives entirely, but also freely and frankly to dismiss them, friendly and courteously entreating your lordships not at all to take it in evil part that you cannot be present at his Majesty's Feast of Honour; but to remember that there in notwithstanding more imposed upon your lordship. by God Almighty (who in the distribution of his gifts hath an incomprehensible consideration) than you can duely and easily sustain. Neither is your reputation hereby prejudiced, although you be rejected by this our order, since we cannot at once all of us, do all things. But for as much as your lordships have been seduced by base rascals, it shall not on their part, pass unrevenged. And furthermore his Majesty resolveth shortly to communicate with your lordships a catalogue of hereticks or* Index Expurgatorius, *that you may hence forward be able with better judgment to discern between the good and the evil. And because his Majesty e're long also purposeth to rummage his library, and offer up the reductive writings to Vulcan, he friendly, humbly, and courteously entreats every one of your lordships to put the name in execution with your own, whereby it is to be hoped that all evil and mischief may for the time to come be remedied. And*

*you are withal to be admonished, never henceforth so inconsiderately to covet*
*an entrance hither, least the former excuse of seducers be taken from you,*
*and you fall into disgrace and contempt of all men. In fine, for as much as*
*the estates of the land have still somewhat to demand of your lordships, his*
*Majesty hopes that no man will think much to redeem himself with a chain*
*or what else he hath about him, and so in friendly manner to depart from us,*
*and through our safe conduct to betake himself home again."*

The others who stood not at the first, third and fourth weight,
his Majesty will not no lightly dismiss. But that they also may now
experience his Majesty's gentleness, it is his command, to strip them
stark naked and so send them forth.

Those who in the second and fifth weight were found too light,
shall besides stripping, be noted with one, two or more brand-marks,
according as each one was lighter, or heavier.

They who were drawn up by the sixth or seventh, and not by the
rest, shall be somewhat more gratiously dealt withal, and so forward.
For unto every combination there was a certain punishment ordained,
which were here too long to recount.

They who yesterday separated themselves freely of their own
accord, shall go at liberty without any blame.

Finally, the convicted vagabond-cheaters who could move up
none of the weights, shall as occasion serves, be punished in body and
life, with the sword, halter, water and rods. And such execution of
judgment shall be inviolably observed for an example unto others.

Herewith our Virgin broke her wand, and the other who read
the sentence, blowed her trumpet, and stepped with most profound
reverence towards those who stood behind the curtain.

But here I cannot omit to discover somewhat to the reader
concerning the number of our prisoners, of whom those who weighed
one, were seven; those who weighed two, were twenty one; they who
three, thirty five; they who four, thirty five; those who five, twenty
one; those who six, seven; but he that came to the seventh, and yet
could not well raise it, he was only one, and indeed the same whom
I released. Besides, of them who wholly failed there were many. But
of those who drew all the weights from the ground, but few. And
these as they stood severally before us, no I diligently numbered, and
noted them down in my table-book. And it is very admirable that

amongst those who weighed any thing, none was equal to another. For although amongst those who weighed three, there were thirty five, yet one of them weighed the first, second, and third, another the third, fourth, and fifth, a third, the fifth, sixth and seventh and so on. It is likewise very wonderful that amongst one hundred and twenty six who weighed any thing, none was equal to another. And I would very willingly name them all, with each mans weight, were it not as yet forbidden me. But I hope it may hereafter be published with the interpretation.

Now this Judgment being read over, the lords in the first place were well satisfied, because in such severity they durst not look for a mild sentence. For which cause they gave more than they were desired, and each one redeemed himself with chains, jewels, gold, monies and other things, as much as they had about them, and with reverence took leave. Now although the King's servants were forbidden to jear any at his going away, yet some unlucky birds could not hold laughing, and certainly it was sufficiently ridiculous to see them pack away with such speed, without once looking behind them. Some desired that the promised catalogue might with the first be dispatched after them, and then they would take such order with their books as should be pleasing to his Majesty; which was again assured. At the door was given to each of them out of a cup a draught of FORGETFULNESS, that so he might have no further memory of misfortune.

After these the voluntiers departed, who because of their ingenuity were suffered to pass, but yet so as never to return again in the same fashion. But if to them (as likewise to the others) any thing further were revealed, then they should become well-come guests.

Meanwhile others were stripping, in which also an inequality (according to each man's demerit) was observ'd. Some were sent away naked, without other hurt. Others were driven out with small bells. Some were scourged forth. In brief the punishments were so various, that I am not able to recount them all. In the end it came to the last also with whom somewhat a longer time was spent, for whilst some were hanging, some beheading, some forced to leap into the water, and the rest otherwise dispatching, much time was consumed. Verily at this execution my eyes ran over, not indeed in regard of the punishment, which they otherwise for their impudency well deserved, but in contemplation of human blindness, in that we are continually busting ourselves in that which ever since the first Fall hath been hitherto sealed up to us. Thus the garden which so lately was quite full, was soon emptied; so that besides the soldier there was not a man left.

Now as soon as this was done, and silence had been kept for the space of five minutes, there came forward a beautiful snow-white unicorn with a golden coller (having it in certain letters) about his neck. In the same place he bowed himself down upon both his fore-feet, as if hereby he had shown honour to the lion, who stood so immoveably upon the fountain, that I took him to be of stone or brass, who immediately took the naked sword which he bare in his paw, and brake it in the middle in two, the piece. whereof to my thinking sunk into the fountain: after which he so long roared, until a white dove brought a branch of olive in her bill, which the lion devoured in an instant, and so was quieted. And so the unicorn returned to his place with joy.

Hereupon our Virgin lead us down again by the winding stairs from the scaffold, and so we again made our reverence toward the curtain. We were to wash our hands and heads in the fountain, and there a little while to wait in our order till the King through a certain secret gallery were again returned into his hall and then we also with choice music, pomp, state and pleasant discourse were conducted into our former lodging. And this was done about four in the afternoon. But that in the meanwhile the time might not seem too long to us, the Virgin bestowed on each of us a noble page, who were not only richly habited, but also exceedingly learned, so that they could so aptly discourse upon all subjects, that we had good reason to be ashamed of our selves. These were commanded to lead us up and down the castle yet but into certain places and if possible, to shorten the time according to our desire. Mean time the Virgin took leave with this consolation, that at supper she would be with us again, and after that celebrate the ceremonies of the hanging up of the weights, requesting that we would in patience waite till the next day, for on the morrow we must be presented to the King.

She being thus departed from us, each of us did what best pleased him. One part viewed the excellent paintings, which they copied out for themselves, and considered also what the wonderful characters might signify. Others were fain to recruit themselves again with meat and drink.

I indeed caused my page to conduct me (together with my companion) up and down the castle, of which walk it will never repent me as long as I have a day to live. For besides many other glorious antiquities, the royal sepulcher was also shewed me, by which I learned more than is extant in all books. There in the same place stands also the glorious Phoenix (of which two years since I published a particular small discourse) and am resolved (in case this my narration shall prove useful) to set forth several and peculiar treatises, concerning the Lion, Eagle, Griffon, Falcon and other like, together with their draughts and inscriptions. It grieves me also for my other conforts, that they neglected such pretious treasures. And yet I cannot but think it was the special will of God it should be so. I indeed reaped the most benefit by my page, for according as each ones genius lay, so he lead his intrusted into the quarters and places which were pleasing to him. Now the keys hereunto belonging were committed to my page, and therefore this good fortune happened to me before the rest; for although he invited others to come in, yet they imagining such tombs to be only in the churchyard, thought they would well enough get thither, when ever any thing was to be seen there. Neither shall these monuments (as both of us copied and transcribed them) be withheld from my thankful scholars.

The other thing that was shewed us two was the noble library as it was altogether before the Reformation. Of which (albeit it rejoices my heart as often as I call it to mind) I have so much the less to say, because the catalogue thereof in very shortly to be published. At the entry of this room stands a great book, the like whereof I never saw, in which all the figures, rooms, portals, also all the writings, riddles ant the like, to be seen in the whole castle, are delineated. Now although we made some promise concerning this also, yet at present I must contain my self, and first learn to know the world better. In every book stands its author painted, whereof (as I understood) many were to be burnt, that so even their memory may be blotted out from amongst the righteous.

Now having taken a full view hereof, and being scarce gotten forth, another page came running to us, and having whispered somewhat in our pages ear, he delivered up the keys to him, who immediately carried them up the winding stair. But our page was very much out of countenance, and we setting hard upon him with entreaties, he declared to us that the King's Majesty would by no means permit that either of the two, namely the library and sepulchers, should be seen by any man and therefore he besought us as we tendered his life, to discover it to no man, he having already utterly denied it. Whereupon both of us stood hovering between joy and fear, yet it continued in silence, and no man made further inquiry about it. Thus in both places we consumed three hours, which does not at all repent me.

Now although it had already struck seven, yet nothing was hitherto given us to eat, howbeit our hunger was easie to be abated by constant revivings, and I could be well content to fast all my life long with such entertainment. About this time the curious fountains, mines, and all kind of art-shops, were also shown us, of which there was none but surpassed all our arts, though they should all be melted into one mass. All their chambers were built in semi-circle, that so they might have before their eyes the costly clock-work which was erected upon a fair turret in the center, and regulate themselves according to the course of the planets, which were to be seen on it in a glorious manner. And hence I could easily conjecture wherein our artists failed, howbeit its none of my duty to inform them.

At length I came into a spacious room (shown indeed to the rest a great while before) in the middle whereof stood a terrestrial globe, whose diameter contained thirty foot, albeit near half of it, except a little which was covered with the steps, was let into the earth. Two men might readily turn this globe about with all its furniture, so that more of it was never to be seen, but so much as was above the horizon. Now although I could easily conceive that this was of some special use, yet could I not understand whereto those ringlets of gold (which were upon it in several places) served; at which my page laughed and advised me to view them more narrowly. In brief, I found there my native country noted with gold also. Whereupon my companion sought his, and found that so too. Now for as much as the same happened in like manner to the rest who stood by, the page told us of a certain that it was yesterday declared to the Kings Majest'y by their old Atlas (so is the astronomer named) that all the gilded points did exactly answer to their native countries, according as had been shown of each of them. And therefore he also, as soon as he perceived that I undervalued my self and that nevertheless there stood a point upon my native country, moved one of the captains to intreat for us, that we should be set upon the scale (without our peril) at all adventures; especially seeing one of our native countries had a notable good mark. And truly it was not without cause that he, the page who had the greatest power of all the rest, was bestowed on me. For this I then returned him thanks, and immediately looked more diligently upon my native country, and found more over that besides the ringlet, there were also certain delicate streaks upon it, which nevertheless I would not be thought to speak to my own praise or glory.

I saw much more too upon this globe than I am willing to discover. Let each man take into consideration why each city produceth not a philosopher. After this he lead us quite into the globe, which was thus made. On the sea was a tablet, whereon stood three dedications, and the author's name, which a man might gently lift up and by a little joyned board, go into the center, which was capable of four persons, being nothing but a round board whereon we could sit and at ease by broad daylight (it was now already dark) contemplate the stars. To my thinking they were mere carbuncles which glittered in an agreeable order, and moved so gallantly, that I had scarce any mind ever to go out again, as the page afterwards told the Virgin, with which she often twitched me.

For it was already supper time, and I had so much amused my self in the globe, that I was almost the last at table; wherefore I made no longer delay, but having again put on my gown (which I had before laid aside) and stepping to the table, the waiters treated me with so much reverence and honour, that for shame I durst not look up, and so unawares permitted the Virgin, who attended me on one side, to stand, which she soon perceiving twitched me by the gown, and so led me to the table. To speak any further concerning the music, or the rest of that magnificent entertainment, I hold it needless both because it is not possible sufficently to express it, and I have above reported it according so my power. In brief, there was nothing there but art and amenity.

Now after we had each to other related our employment since

noon (howbeit, not a word was spoken of the library and monuments) being already merry with the wine the Virgin began thus: "*My lords, I have a great contention with one of my sisters. In our chamber we have an eagle. Now we cherish him with such diligence. that each of us in desirous to be the best beloved, and upon that score have many a squabble. On a day we concluded to go both together to him, and toward whom he should show himself most friendly, hers should he properly be; this we did. and I (as commonly) bare in my hand a branch of laurel, but my sister had none. Now as soon as he espied us both, he immediately gave my sister another branch which he had in his beak, and offered at mine, which I gave him. Now each of us hereupon imagined her self to be best beloved of him. Which way am I to resolve my self?*"

This modest proposal of the Virgin pleased us all mighty well and each one would gladly have heard the solution, but in as much as they all looked upon me. and desired to have the beginning from me, my mind was so extremely confounded that I knew not what else to do with it but propound another in its stead. and therefore said, "*Gracious Lady, your ladyships question were easily to be resolved if one thing did not perplex me. I had two companions, both which loved me exceedingly; now they being doubtful which of them was most dear to me, concluded to run to me unaware, and that he whom I should then embrace should be the right; this they did, yet one of them could not keep pace with the other, so he staid behind and wept; the other I embraced with amazement. Now when they had afterwards discovered the business to me, I knew not how to resolve myself and have hitherto let it rest in this manner, until I may find some good advice herein.*"

The Virgin wondered at it, and well observed where about I was. whereupon she replied, "*well then let us both be quit,*" and then desired the solution from the rest.

But I had already made them wise. Whereupon the next began thus: "*In the city where I live, a virgin was lately condemned to death, but the judge being something pitiful towards her, caused it to be proclaimed that if any man desired to become the virgin's champion, he should have free leave to do it. Now she had two lovers; the one presently made himself ready, and came into the lists to expect his adversary; afterwards the other also presented himself. but coming somewhat too late, he resolved nevertheless to fight, and willingly suffer himself to be vanquished, that so the virgin's life might be* preserved, which also succeeded accordingly."

Whereupon each challenged her: "*Now my lords instruct me, to which of them of right belongeth she?*"

The Virgin could hold no longer, but said, "*I thought to have gained much information, and am my self gotten into the net but yet would gladly hear whether there be any more behind.*"

"*Yes, that there is,*" answered a third, "*a stranger adventure hath not been yet recounted than that which happened to my self. In my youth I loved a worthy maid. Now that this my love might attain its wished end, I was fain to make use of an ancient matron, who easily brought me to her. Now it happened that the maid's brethren came in upon us just as we three were together, who were in such a rage that they would have taken my life, but upon my vehement supplication, they at length forced me to swear to take each of them for a year, to my wedded wife. Now tell me my lords, should I take the old, or the young one first?*"

We all laughed sufficiently at this riddle, and although some of them muttered one to another thereupon, yet none would undertake to unfold it.

Hereupon the fourth began; "*In a certain city there dwelt an honourable lady, who was beloved of all, but especially by a young noble man, who would needs be too importunate with her; at length she gave him this determination, that in case he would, in a cold winter, lead her into a fair green garden of roses, then he should obtain, but if not, he must resolve never to see her more. The noble man travelled into all countries to find such a man as might perform this, till at length he lite upon a little old man that promised to do it for him, in case he would assure him of half his estate, which he having consented to the other was as good as his word. Whereupon he invited the aforesaid lady to his garden, where contrary to her expectation, she found all things green, pleasant and warm, and withal remembering her promise, she only requested that she might once more return to her lord, to whom with sighs and tears she bewailed her lamentable condition. But for as much as he sufficiently perceived her faithfulness, he dispatched her back to her lover, who had so dearly purchased her, so that she might give him satisfaction. This husband's integrity did so mightily affect the noble man, that he thought it a sin to touch so honest a wife; so he sent her home again with honour to her lord. Now the little man perceiving such faith in both these, would not, how poor soever he were, be the least, but restored the noble man all his goods again and went his way. Now my lords, I know not which of these persons may have shown the greatest ingenuity?"*

Here our tongues were quite cut off. Neither would the Virgin make any other reply, but only that another should go on.

Wherefore the fifth, without delay, began: *"My Lords, I desire not to make long work; who hath the greater joy, he that beholdeth what he loveth, Or he that only thinketh on it?"*

*"He that beholdeth it,"* said the Virgin.

*"Nay"* answered I.

Hereupon arose a contest, wherefore the sixth called out, *"My lords, I am to take a wife; now I have before me a maid, a married wife, and a widow; ease me of this doubt, and I will afterwards help to order the rest."*

*"It goes well there,"* replied the seventh, *"where a man hath his choice, but with me the case is otherwise; in my youth I loved a fair and virtuous virgin from the bottom of my heart, and she me in like manner: howbeit because of her friends denial we could not come together in wedlock. Whereupon she was married to another, yet an honest and discreet person, who maintained her honourably and with affection, until she came into the pains of child-birth, which went so hard with her that all thought she had been dead, so with much state, and great mourning she was interred. Now I thought with my self, during her life thou couldst have no part in this woman, but yet now dead as she is thou mayst embrace and kiss her sufficiently; whereupon I took my servant with me, who dug her up by night. Now having opened the coffin and locked her in my arms, and feeling about her heart, I found still some little motion in it, which increased more and more from my warmth, till at last I perceived that she was indeed still alive; wherefore I quietly bare her home. and after I had warmed her chilled body with a costly bath of herbs, I committed her to my mother until she brought forth a fair son, whom (as the mother) I caused faithfully to be nursed. After two days (she being then in a mighty amazement) I discovered to her all the forepassed affair, requesting her that for the time to come she would live with me as a wife, against which she thus excepted, in case it should be grievous to her husband who had well and honourably maintained her. But if it could otherwise be, she was the present obliged in love to one as well as the other. Now after two months (being then to make a journey elsewhere) I invited her husband as a guest, and amongst other things demanded of him, whether if his deceased wife should come home again, he could be content to receive*

her, and he affirming it with tears and lamentations, at length I brought him his wife together with his son, and an account of all the forepassed business, intreating him to ratifie with his consent my fore-purposed espousals. After a long dispute he could not beat me from my right, but was fain to leave me the wife. But still the contest was about the son."

Here the Virgin interrupted him, and said, "*It makes me wonder how you could double the afflicted mans grief.*"

"*How,*" answered he, "*was I not then concerned?*"

Upon this there arose a dispute amongst us, yet the most part affirmed that he had done but right.

"*Nay,*" said he, "*I freely returned him both his wife and son. Now tell me my lords, was my honesty, or this man's joy the greater?*"

These words had so much cheered the Virgin that (as if it had been for the sake of these two) she caused a health to be drunk.

After which the rest of the proposals went on somewhat perplexedly, so that I could not retain them all, yet this comes to my mind, that one said, that a few years before he had seen a physician, who bought a parcel of wood against winter, with which he warmed himself all winter long; but as soon as the spring returned he sold the very same wood again, and so had the use of it for nothing.

"*Here must needs be skill,*" said the Virgin, "*but the time is now past.*"

"*Yea,*" replied my companion, "*who ever understands not how to resolve all the riddles, may give each man notice of it by a proper messenger, I conceive he will not be denied.*"

At this time they began to say grace, and we arose altogether from the table, rather satisfied and merry than glutted; and it were to be wished that all invitations and feastings were thus to be kept. Having now taken some few turns up and down the hall again, the Virgin asked us whether we desired to begin the wedding.

"*Yes,*" said one, "*noble and virtuous lady.*" Whereupon she privately dispatched a page, and yet in the mean time proceeded in discourse with us. In brief she was already become so familiar with us, that I adventured and requested her Name. The Virgin smiled at my curiosity, but yet was not moved, but replied:

"*My Name contains five and fifty, and yet hath only eight letters; the third is the third part of the fifth, which added to the sixth will produce a number whose root shall exceed the third itself by just the first, and it is the half of the fourth. Now the fifth and the seventh are equal, the last and the first are also equal, and make with the second as much as the sixth hath, which contains just four more than the third tripled. Now tell me, my lord, how am I called?"*[1]

The answer was intricate enough to me, yet I left not off so, but said, noble and virtuous lady, may I not obtain one only letter? Yea, said she, that may well be done. What then (replied I again) may the seventh contain? It contains (said she) as many as there are lords here. With this I was content, and easily found her Name, at which she was well pleased, with assurance that much more should yet be revealed to us.

Mean time certain virgins had made themselves ready, and came in with great ceremony. First of all two youths carried lights before them; one of them was of jocund countenance, sprightly eyes and gentile proportion. The other looks something angerly, and whatever he would have, must be, as I afterwards perceived. After them first followed four virgins. One looked shame-facedly towards the earth, very humble in behaviour. The second also was a modest, bashful virgin. The third, as she entered the room seemed amazed at somewhat, and as I understood, she cannot well abide where there is too much mirth. The fourth brought with her certain small wreaths, thereby to manifest her kindness and liberality.

After these four came two which were somewhat more gloriously apparelled; they saluted us courteously. One of them had a gown of sky colour spangled with golden stars. The others was green, beautified with red and white stripes. On their heads they had thin flying tissaties, which did most becomingly adorn them.

---

[1] The answer to this riddle was first proposed by Leibnitz who had an interest in Rosicrucianism: (Adam McLean, *Commentary on the Chymical Wedding*, Edinburgh 1984, p.88).

The problem arising from this was clearly a discrepancy in the total. Whilst the name "Alchimia" is entirely apt, it doesn't add up to 55 according to the formula opposite. Perhaps a printing error crept in some-where and was perpetuated in following editions.

| | | |
|---|---|---|
| 1st letter | 1 = | A |
| 2nd letter | 12 = | L |
| 3rd letter | 3 = | C |
| 4th letter | 8 = | H |
| 5th letter | 9 = | I |
| 6th letter | 13 = | M |
| 7th letter | 9 = | I |
| 8th letter | 1 = | A |
| | 56 | |

At last came one alone, who had on her head a coronet, but rather looked up towards heaven, than towards earth. We all thought it had been the Bride, but were much mistaken, although otherwise in honour, riches and state she much surpassed the Bride; and she afterwards ruled the whole Wedding. Now on this occasion we all followed our Virgin, and fell down on our knees, howbeit she showed her self extreme humble, offering every one her hand, and admonishing us not to be too much surprised at this, for this was one of her smallest bounties, but to lift up our eye to our Creator, and learn hereby to acknowledge his omnipotency, and so proceed in our enterprised course, employing this grace to the praise to God, and the good of man. In sum, her words were quite different from those of our Virgin, who was somewhat more worldly. They pierced even through my bones and marrow.

"*And thou,*" said she further to me, "*hast received more than others, see that thou also make a larger return.*" This to me was a very strange sermon; for as soon a. we saw the virgins with the music, we imagined we must presently fall to dancing, but that time was not as yet come. Now the weights, whereof mention has been before made, stood still in the same place, wherefore the Queen (I yet knew not who she was) commanded each virgin to take up one, but to our Virgin she gave her own, which was the last and greatest, and commanded us to follow behind. Our majesty was then somewhat abated, for I well observed that our Virgin was but too good for us, and we were not so highly reputed as we our selves wore almost in part willing to fantasy. So we went behind in our order, and were brought into the first chamber, where our Virgin in the first place hung up the Queen's weight, during which an excellent spiritual hymn was sung. There was nothing costly in this room save only curious little prayer books which should never be missing. In the midst was erected a pulpit, very convenient for prayer, where in the Queen kneeled down, and about her we were all fain to kneel and pray after the Virgin, who read out of a book, that this Wedding might tend to the honour of God, and our own benefit. Afterwards we came into the second chamber, where the first Virgin hung up her weight also, and so forward until all the ceremonies were finished. Hereupon the Queen again presented her hand to every one, and departed thence with her virgin.

Our president stayed yet a while with us. But because it had been already two hours night, she would no longer detain us; me thought she was glad of our company, yet she bid us good night, and wished us quiet rest, and so departed friendly, although unwillingly from us. Our pages were well instructed in their business, and therefore showed every man his chamber, and stayed also with us in another pallet that in case we wanted any thing we might make use of them My chamber (of the rest I am not able to speak) was royally furnished with rare tapestries and hung about with paintings. But above all things I delighted in my page, who was so excellently spoken. and experienced in the arts, that he yet spent another hour with me and it was half an hour after three when first I fell asleep. And this indeed was the first night that I slept in quiet, and yet a scurvy dream would not suffer me to rest; for I was all the night troubled with a door which I could not get open. but at last I did it. With these fantasies I passed the time. till at length cowards day I awaked.